# THE YANGTZE RIVER

*Books by Margaret Rau*

THE YANGTZE RIVER
THE YELLOW RIVER
THE PENGUIN BOOK
THE BAND OF THE RED HAND
DAWN FROM THE WEST:
*The Story of Genevieve Caulfield*

# THE
# YANGTZE
# RIVER

*Margaret Rau*

*Illustrated with photographs*

JULIAN MESSNER  NEW YORK

*To my godson,*
*John Thomas Auyong*

Published simultaneously in the United States and Canada by Julian Messner, a division of Simon & Schuster, Inc., 1 West 39 Street, New York, N.Y. 10018. All rights reserved.

*Photo Credits*

*From the Award-Winning Television Documentary, China: The Roots of Madness: p. 30, 71*

*From China: Empire of 700 Million by Harry Hamm, translated by Victor Anderson. Copyright © 1966 by Harry Hamm. Reprinted by permission of Doubleday & Company, Inc.: p. 27, 33(left), 54(bottom), 58, 59, 66, 76, 82*

*Gest Oriental Library and Far Eastern Collections of Princeton University: p. 8, 20, 33(right), 37, 45, 61, 64*

*Library of Congress: p. 34*

*Northwest Airlines: p. 73*

*Office of Tibet: p. 10, 11, 13, 15, 16, 18, 19*

*United Press International: p. 26, 28, 44, 47, 49, 52, 67, 74, 75*

*U.S. Air Force: p. 25*

*U.S. Army: p. 80*

*Wide World Photos: p. 85, 86*

*Printed in the United States of America*

ISBN 0-671-32335-0 Cloth Trade
0-671-32336-9 MCE
Library of Congress Catalog Card No. 76-123558

DESIGN BY: SUE CROOKS

# CONTENTS

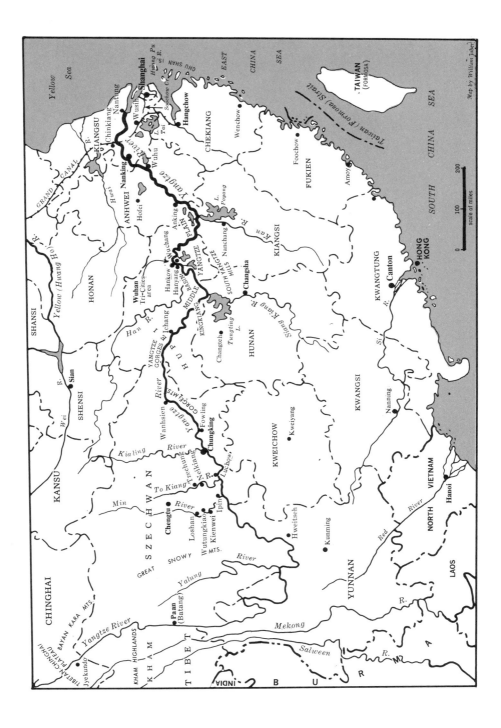

Map by William Jaber

Yellow Sea

CHU SHAN IS.

Hwang Pu R.

Soochow Cr.

EAST CHINA SEA

TAIWAN (FORMOSA)

Taiwan (Formosa) Strait

SOUTH CHINA SEA

scale of miles
0    100    200

KANSU
KIANGSU
Chinkiang
GRAND CANAL
Huai R.
ANHWEI
Nanning
Nanking
Wusih
Shanghai
Hofei
L. Tai
Hangchow
CHEKIANG
Wenchow
FUKIEN
Foochow
Amoy

SHANSI
HONAN
Yellow (Hwang Ho) R.
Wuchang
Anking
Yangtze River
YANGTZE PLAIN
L. Poyang
Kan R.
Nanchang
KIANGSI
KWANGTUNG
Canton
HONG KONG

Wei R.
Sian
SHENSI
Wuhan
Tri-Cities area
Hankow
Hanyang
Han R.
MIDDLE YANGTZE BASIN
KINGKIANG
SOUTH YANGTZE HILLS
Tungting L.
Changteh
Changsha
HUNAN
Siang Kiang R.
Si R.
KWANGSI
Nanning

YANGTZE GORGES
Ichang
HUPEH
Wanhsien
Yangtze River
Fowling
GORGE MTS.
Chungking
Kialing River
To Kiang
Tzechung
N. R.
Luchow
Luchow
KWEICHOW
Kweiyang
NORTH VIETNAM
Hanoi

KANSU
Min
SZECHWAN
Neikiang
Chengtu
River
Loshan
Wutungkiao
Kienwei
Iping
Hweitseh
GREAT SNOWY MTS.
Yalung River
Kunming
YUNNAN
Red River
LAOS

CHINGHAI
BAYAN KARA MTS.
Jyekundo
Paan (Batang)
KHAM HIGHLANDS
TSINGHAI PLATEAU
TIBETAN PLATEAU
Yangtze River
KHAM
Yalung
TIBET
Mekong
Salween
R.
BURMA
INDIA

## CHAPTER 1

# THE WILD FEMALE YAK RIVER

Greatest of all the rivers of Asia is the Yangtze Kiang. It rushes out of central Asia to twist like a great red serpent for thirty-six hundred miles across China to the Pacific Ocean far to the east.

The river begins its journey in the Kokoshili Mountains, which rise out of the largest plateau in the world, the Tibetan-Chinghai plateau. The southwestern part of this plateau lies in the country of Tibet. The northeastern part of it belongs to the Chinese province of Chinghai. But most of the people who live on the plateau are Tibetans.

The Yangtze has many different names along its course. The Tibetans call it the Dri Chu, which means Wild Female Yak River. The name comes from a legend told in ancient

7

times. It said that a huge, long-haired female yak stood in the mysterous mountains of the west with its mouth forever open. From over its drooping red tongue, the waters of the great river came pouring down.

At the Yangtze's source, the peaks of the Kokoshili range are always blanketed in snow. The mountain slopes are sheeted with cold blue glaciers that glitter in the frosty light. In winter, blizzards howl without stopping and the land and water are frozen solid.

*Frozen snow and ice cover the headwaters of the Yangtze River and glaciers sheet the surrounding mountain slopes.*

But spring brings a gentler air. The snow begins to melt. The ice thaws, and water trickles over the faces of the glaciers. In clefts and deep canyons, there is the sound of cascading brooks and rivulets, all making their way downward. From a hundred different directions, these waters enter the desolate plain below and meander across it, uniting one by one until a single giant stream is formed. This is the young Yangtze Kiang. Its waters are icy cold and crystal clear.

All around, as far as the eye can see, low hills roll like the waves of a vast sea. The shallow valleys between the hills are soggy with marshes and strewn with small salt lakes. Here and there, giant ice cones stand like ghostly pillars. They are geysers of hot water that have been frozen by the intense cold.

This dreary region, some eighteen thousand feet above sea level, is too high and cold for trees. Only small bushes and patches of yellow needle-sharp grass grow here. Man cannot live in such desolate wastes, but many animals do. Antelope, wild sheep and asses roam far and wide in search of the sparse pasturage.

Thundering herds of yaks, distant cousins of the American bison, often visit the Yangtze to drink its fresh sweet waters. The yaks are covered with long thick hair, which protects them against the cold. But they almost suffocate on warmer days. When the sun is shining, they plunge into the river for a cooling swim.

But the Yangtze doesn't always treat its visitors kindly.

*Long-haired yak can live on the desolate Tibetan-Chinghai plateau.*

A sudden drop in temperature may freeze the water almost instantly. Then the unwary animals are caught in a block of solid ice.

For nearly two hundred miles, the Yangtze flows in an easterly direction through the desolate land. Then the Bayan Kara mountain range blocks the river's course and turns it southward. Here, it is joined by two other rivers which are also on their way to the sea. One is the Yellow River, which curls across North China and empties into the Gulf of Po Hai. The other is the Mekong River, which has begun a journey that will take it down into Southeast Asia and the South China Sea.

Between these two rivers, the Yangtze meanders down a broad, shallow valley. As it descends through Chinghai Province, it enters the pasture lands of the nomad peoples who roam the plains with their flocks and herds.

In the winter, when deep snow covers the ground and

the ponds and rivers are frozen on the higher plateau, the nomads have to move to lower altitudes. But in the late spring and summer, when the snow melts, rains and warm sunlight transform the mountain slopes and valleys to green meadow lands splattered with gay flowers. Then the nomads return to their homes, driving their yak herds before them.

The yaks provide the nomads with plenty of rich milk. But Tibetans do not drink their milk fresh. The buckets used for milking are never washed, and the stale milk which coats them immediately turns fresh milk sour. But the Tibetans regard sour-milk curds as a delicacy. They also make cheese, and butter which is always rancid. They like to melt great lumps of strong-tasting butter in their tea to make tea soup.

The nomad men are tall and dark. They look gigantic

*A nomad encampment that has moved to a lower altitude is prepared for the winter.*

sitting atop their small ponies as they ride herd on the yak. Their black hair hangs to their shoulders or is wound around their heads in thick braids. Great silver earrings ornamented with coral or turquoise swing in their ears. Many of them wear large felt hats, and all of them have boots with bright green or red leggings.

They are clad in only one garment—a long cloak which is called a *shuba*. A shuba is made of seven sheepskins which are first tanned in butter and then stitched together with the fleece turned in for warmth. The long robe would reach the floor, but a belt is fastened around the waist to draw it up and make a deep blouse so that the skirt falls just below the knees.

In the blouse of his shuba, the nomad stores all the necessities of life on the road—an eating bowl, some roasted barley flour, tea, a pouch of rancid butter, a knife, and a flint to start fires.

The nomad women also wear boots and shubas. Their hair is plaited with brightly colored wool yarn which hangs below the waist in a long fringed tassel. They wear gay necklaces of coral, turquoise, and huge amber beads.

The women, with the help of great black mastiffs, shepherd the flocks of goats and sheep. Showing their teeth and barking fiercely, the dogs rush up to straying animals and with sharp nips bring them back to the herd.

Children, in oversize shubas and fur caps, run barefoot everywhere.

Finally, the nomads reach their encampment and pitch

*These nomad women wear long shubas that are belted at the waist. Their hair is braided with colored wool yarns.*

their great black tents. With people bustling about everywhere, the land takes on a friendly, lively look. At night, they sing and dance by the light of their bonfires.

Down through the lands of the nomads, the Yangtze flows. As it continues to descend, tiny vegetable gardens of hardy turnips and peas appear in sheltered places.

Presently the gardens turn into small fields of barley. Soon the fields grow larger. Adobe farmhouses, with flat roofs and tiny slits for windows, cluster among the fields. On the hillsides, herds of yaks, sheep, and goats graze.

Occasionally, steep bluffs crowd down to the banks of the river. Then travelers have to make their way along the narrow foot trail that is cut into the face of the cliffs. Below them, the river rushes along. It is no longer crystal clear, but muddy from its journey through the red soil of the Chinghai plateau.

The Yangtze is almost seven hundred feet wide now and so turbulent that it can no longer be safely forded even on horseback. To cross from one side to the other, travelers have to go by ferry.

But the ferries are not like those with which you are familiar. They are wickerwork baskets about six feet in diameter, covered with yak skins. This kind of boat is called a coracle. It looks frail, but it can safely carry a load of luggage and several passengers.

Skill is required, however, to manage a coracle. The helmsman—his long hair wound round his head like a turban, his shuba tucked well above his knees—uses a long wooden paddle. He steers the boat into the swift current, then lets it ride downstream, bobbing like an eggshell through flying spray and choppy waves. Finally, he is able to bring it safely to the opposite shore, but he may be several miles below his starting point.

Leaving the ferryman to carry his coracle back upstream for another load, the Yangtze rushes on. But about four hundred miles from its source, it slows its pace. Along this section, low mountains border the river to the west. On the other side of the mountains, and out of sight, is the ancient town of Jyekundo, or Yushu as it is called by the Chinese.

In early days, Jyekundo was a great center for trade between China and Tibet. It lay on the Old Tea Road, which led from Szechwan Province in the east to the Tibetan capital of Lhasa in the west. The road crossed the

*Travelers with their bundles piled high wait patiently for the ferry at the crossing.*

*The boat hurrying towards the ferry landing is called a coracle. Made of yakskins stretched across wickerwork baskets, it can carry passengers and luggage quite safely.*

Yangtze at this point and then climbed over the mountains to Jyekundo. It was called the Old Tea Road because of the great quantities of tea that were shipped over it.

Every summer, Chinese porters used to carry the tea up the steep stone staircases which led out of Szechwan Province. Here, the tea was loaded onto yaks. When the caravan came to the Yangtze, the yaks had to swim across it to reach Jyekundo. Then the river was black with thousands of yaks all bearing great loads of tea bricks packed in yak skins.

Today, yaks are not used for caravan work. There is no longer any need for them. Tea for the Tibetans now comes over a new highway in great convoys of trucks.

Left: *A nomad herdsman guards the bundles that will be loaded onto the yaks.* Right: *These Tibetan nomads are transporting goods by yak.*

## CHAPTER 2

# THE RIVER OF GOLDEN SAND

Beyond Jyekundo, the Yangtze continues through pleasant valley lands, with rocky hills and marshes scattered here and there. The villages are larger than those on the upper reaches of the river. Many of the flat-roofed houses here are two storied. The first story has an open front and is used as a barn. When the weather is freezing, yaks, sheep, and goats are herded into the barn for warmth.

The second story is the living quarters for several families. It has narrow slits for windows and is reached by an outside staircase or a ladder. The flat roof is used for drying things. In the summer, all the village roofs are covered with hundreds of turnips which have been laid out to dry. When the turnips are ready, they will be packed into barrels and put away until cold winter evenings come. Then

*The flat roofs of these two-storied Tibetan houses are used for drying things. Several families live in the second story; the first story is used as a barn for animals and storage.*

they will be brought out and cooked and eaten with hot buttered tea and dough balls made of roasted barley flour, which the Tibetans call *tsamba*.

Occasionally, one can see the fortress-like walls of an ancient lamasery clinging to the side of a mountain or on the top of a hill above the villages. A lamasery is a Tibetan religious center in which priests, who are called lamas, live and conduct their services. Before the 1950's, hundreds, even thousands, of lamas lived in each lamasery. The farmlands of the Tibetan-Chinghai plateau were divided among the lamaseries and the Tibetan noblemen. The peasants worked the fields for them. Then, in 1948, the communists came to power in China. They soon became strong enough to take over all of Tibet. They promised the noblemen and the lamas that they would not interfere with their property rights if they accepted the rule of China. Life went along just about as usual in Tibet.

But, in 1959, there was an uprising against China. The Chinese claimed it was led by the lamas and the noblemen. In order to break their power, the government took away their land and gave it to the people.

Without land, the lamaseries could no longer support the lamas. Only the old priests stayed behind to conduct services in the temples. The young men went out into the world to work. Their former living quarters are now being used as schoolrooms.

Though today the Tibetan peasants own the land which they once farmed as serfs, they do not have individual fields. Instead, the whole village owns the land surrounding it. The herds of yaks, goats, and sheep that graze on the higher ground also belong to everyone. This is the Communist Chinese way of doing things.

The villagers manage their own affairs. They divide themselves into work teams. Some teams tend the fields. Others herd the livestock. Even old women and children

*This ancient building on top of the hill is a lamasery, a religious center for Tibetan priests.*

*The Potala Palace in Lhasa, capital of Tibet, sits majestically on a hill overlooking the city.*

work. They collect fertilizer from the rich dank swamps and manure from the sheep pens and carry it to the fields to feed the crops.

The hardest work of all is in the fall after the harvests are in. Then the work brigades get together to reclaim wastelands. The villagers know that anything they do to increase their crops means a better standard of living for them.

Teams of peasants swarm over the barren, rock-strewn hill slopes. It is so cold at this time of year that the river and marshes are all frozen solid. But the Tibetan men are hardy. Even on freezing days, they strip to the waist, and their backs stream with sweat as they work away.

Since they have no machinery, everything must be done by hand. Some of the men dig out big boulders with pickaxes. Others cart the boulders downhill on carrying poles—two men to the larger boulders. Some of the rocks are so heavy that the men are bent almost double under their weight.

The frozen swamplands at the foot of the hill are dotted with smoky bonfires. Small children scurry from bonfire to bonfire with baskets of dried yak-chips, the Tibetan fuel. They dump the chips onto the fires to keep them going. When their baskets are empty, they rush off to collect another load.

The heat from the bonfires thaws the ground, so men with pickaxes can loosen the swamp earth. Then long processions of men, women, and older children cart the rich soil off in wicker baskets. Up the hill they trudge to spread the soil over the sandy slopes—back and forth, back and forth.

By spring, there is a new field to be sowed, or perhaps a young orchard of apple trees to be planted. In time, there will be little orchards marching in straight rows up hills that once were sandy wastes.

Past the reclaimed hillsides and waving fields of barley, the Yangtze River hurries, gaining more and more speed with every mile. Presently, it leaves the open countryside behind and plunges into the mountainous wilderness of Kham.

It rushes along through deep dark canyons, its course

21

marking the long boundary between China and Tibet. Peaks white with snow tower high overhead, their northern sides blue with glaciers. The winds that blow from them are biting cold. Their lower slopes are so thickly covered with giant pine, fir, and spruce that the branches of the trees let through only a few shafts of sunlight.

The woods are noisy with chattering squirrels. Racoons tumble and play in the green shadows. Badgers haunt the brooks. If a traveler is lucky, he may even catch a glimpse of the rare Golden Monkey, its beautiful fur glimmering in the sunlight, its snub-nosed blue face looking curiously down at him. There are larger animals as well: leopards, bears, and timid deer.

Along this area, the river changes from its normally rich red shade to a deep gold. Through steep canyons and more open valleys, it boils along like a dragon glittering in the sunlight.

The color is caused by millions of flakes of gold. For centuries, the river has been ripping gold out of the mountains and carrying it downstream in the summer floods. In autumn, when the floods recede, they leave long bars of sparkling sand and glittering sand dunes behind. That is why along these stretches the Chinese name for the river is Chinsha Kiang, the River of Golden Sand.

Every fall, when the river shrank, Chinese prospectors used to come with their sieves, shovels, and wooden troughs to pan for gold. But their work never proved profitable, for the flakes are too minute to be gathered easily.

Now, teams of government surveyors have located rich lodes in the surrounding mountains. Today, instead of panning for gold in the river, men dig for it in the earth.

At one point in this lonely wilderness, the golden river is spanned by a steel bridge. Trucks filled with goods and buses crowded with passengers rumble over it. The bridge is part of the highway from Lhasa to Chengtu, capital of Szechwan Province.

At the side of the highway where it crosses the river, there is a little log hut. There are similar huts stationed at intervals along this road, which, during its course, snakes over fourteen mountain ranges and bridges more than a dozen rushing rivers. The huts shelter maintenance crews and their bulldozers. When the spring floods wash earth and rocks onto the highway, the men clear away the debris. When avalanches of snow bury the highway or blizzards cover it with drifts, out come the bulldozers again.

The Lhasa to Chengtu highway is the only modern thoroughfare to be found in this wild country of Kham. In its uplands, live the independent Khamba tribesmen. They raise a few crops of barley in sheltered valleys, but their chief riches are their herds of yaks.

The Khamba tribesmen are Tibetans. In 1959, they took part in the revolt against China. Though Chinese soldiers put down the revolt, the Chinese have never been able to make friends with the Khamba tribesmen. Even today, Chinese are careful about venturing into the Kham wilderness alone.

## CHAPTER 3

# SOUTH OF THE CLOUDS

About six hundred and fifty miles from Jyekundo, the Yangtze enters the province of Yunnan in South China. Here, the river turns abruptly north again, flowing through a deep V-shaped valley between towering mountains. These are the Great Snowy Mountains, which border the Yangtze's eastern bank during its journey south. After the river completes its V-shaped bend, it continues across northern Yunnan in the same zigzag pattern. It can not follow a straight line here because the land is so badly broken by mountains and deep ravines.

Though Yunnan Province lies near the tropics, it is not hot and steamy. This is because it is on a high plateau. The province's many clear days give it its name, Yunnan, which means South of the Clouds.

In the mountains along this section of the Yangtze live

black-haired, black-eyed people who do not belong to the Chinese race. Once, they occupied the whole of the plateau, but, long ago, immigrating Chinese crowded them out of the flat lands. Today, they live mostly in mountainous areas. The Chinese call them the Minority Peoples.

There are the Nasi, whose villages are tucked away in the deep mountain valleys. Nasi women dress in long flared skirts and stiff bonnets that make them look like Dutch peasant women. The Nasi men are fine silversmiths. They get the silver ore from the mountains, and though they find very little, it is enough for their needs. Sitting in their doorways, they hammer out bracelets, brooches, and earrings for sale in the big cities.

The little Miao people cultivate mountain farms here. They love to wear bright-colored clothes, and they look like pink and purple butterflies as they work their land.

*The magnificent towering peaks and deep valleys of the Great Snowy Mountains border the banks of the Yangtze.*

The swarthy Lisu are also farmers. But the proud Yi men who swagger about in full black capes and turbans are horse breeders.

The Mohammadan farmers look the most like Chinese. They are the descendants of Arab traders who first came to China as early as 100 B.C. These traders married Chinese women, and many of them settled in Yunnan Province.

The Communist Chinese do everything they can to keep the Minority Peoples satisfied because if they are unhappy, they will rebel. In former years, there were several serious uprisings of Minority Peoples, especially the spirited Mohammadan Chinese.

As the Yangtze continues eastward, it is joined by the Yalung, a large tributary which flows down from the

*Many of the Minority Peoples of tropical Yunnan cultivate corn and cabbage-like plants on their mountain farms.*

*Miao woman and her child (holding a balloon) on their way to market.*

north. Swollen with the Yalung's waters, the Yangtze rushes along. Now it moves between cliff walls, where little villages perch on jutting ledges, and through open valleys.

In one of these valleys is the highway which leads from Kunming, capital of Yunnan, to Chengtu. In the old days, travelers in this area would have passed stretches of beautiful pink and white poppy fields. These were opium poppies.

Opium was introduced to China in the 1800's by the British, who brought it from India. Its use spread rapidly, until soon thousands and thousands of Chinese were smoking it. They then discovered that they did not have to depend on India for their opium. They could grow it themselves in Szechwan and Yunnan provinces. Soon there were extensive fields of opium in both these provinces.

Since opium was now so easy to get, almost everyone in Yunnan began to smoke it: rich merchants, government officials, bank employees, school children, and peasants. Mothers rubbed it on sugarcane and gave it to their babies as a pacifier. Porters carrying loads from city to city brought their opium kits along and smoked whenever they stopped for a rest.

Opium smokers are never satisfied with just a little. They keep wanting more and more. This kind of craving is called addiction. Smoking opium makes people listless, and working becomes difficult for them.

People became poor and went into debt to buy opium. Then they had to sell their children to pay their debts. There were thousands of child slaves in old Yunnan. They were usually treated harshly by their masters. Many were put to work in tin, coal, and copper mines in the province.

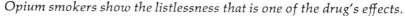

*Opium smokers show the listlessness that is one of the drug's effects.*

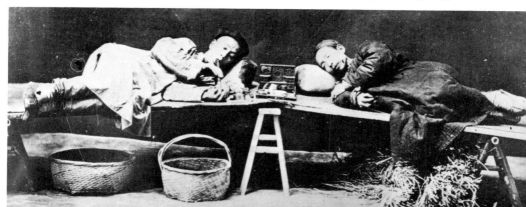

After a few years, they died of starvation or overwork, but their owners did not care. There were always plenty of others to take their places.

Today, opium is forbidden in China, and there are no more opium fields. The children no longer work the mines. Now, adults dig the coal, tin, and copper, which is then sent by truck or train to the new factories that have sprung up in Yunnan Province. Here, farm implements and cooking utensils are manufactured for the peasants of Yunnan, or for export to Southeast Asia.

At the little town of Hweitseh, the Yangtze makes its last bend to the north. Here, it plunges again between towering canyon walls. Along this stretch, there are only a few places where it can be crossed by ferryboat or suspension bridge.

The bridges are made of planks which are fastened together and then hung above the rushing water by chains anchored to either bank. When the wind hurtles through the canyon, the bridges rock to and fro. Even the weight of crossing passengers makes them sway.

The people in this vicinity will show a visitor one of the ferry crossings, at the little town of Chiaochetu near Hweitseh. And they will tell him about the important part it played during the long civil war between the Communist forces led by Mao Tsetung and the Nationalist forces led by Chiang Kaishek.

Mao Tsetung and Chiang Kaishek each had his own plans for reforming China. Chiang Kaishek wanted to go at it slowly so as not to offend the businessmen or the big landlords. By this time, the landlords owned much of the land, and they were renting it to peasants at high fees.

Mao Tsetung wanted immediate reforms. Wherever he went, he promised the peasants he would take the land away from the landlords and give it to them. The peasants flocked to him. But Chiang Kaishek had most of the guns, ammunition, and experienced soldiers.

For several years, the forces of the two men fought each other in South China. But by October of 1934, it looked as though the communists were about to be destroyed. Their

*Left: A youthful Mao Tsetung urges his communist followers to greater efforts in the 1930's. Right: Millions of Chinese peasants, living in poverty and misery, flocked to Mao's teachings.*

only hope was to escape to the north and join their other forces at Yenan in Kansu Province. That was going to be difficult because Chiang Kaishek's troops had almost completely surrounded them.

With ninety thousand followers, some of them women and children, Mao Tsetung retreated across China into Yunnan Province. There, the communists were stopped at the Yangtze because Chiang Kaishek's troops held all the bridges.

One dark night, a few daring Communist soldiers managed to capture the ferry crossing at Chiaochetu. They seized all the ferryboats, and the Communist forces were ferried across the river before Chiang Kaishek's troops could reach them.

Then began the long arduous trek north, through the towering mountains of the Great Snowy range and the desolate Great Grass Wilderness of the Bayan Kara. Many died along the way. Others were killed by Chiang Kaishek's pursuing army or by wild Tibetan tribesmen. When Mao and his southern army finally reached the north and safety, only seven thousand were left of the ninety thousand who had set out.

The communists call this march the Long March, or the March of Ten Thousand Miles. All the school children on mainland China today are familiar with the tales of the heroes who took part in it. They are urged to pattern their lives after these devoted revolutionaries. And many times, classes of school children are brought to look at the ferry crossing, which is now considered a national monument.

# CHAPTER 4

# THE RED BASIN

For two hundred and fifty miles, the Yangtze rushes directly north through the same gigantic sunless canyons. Then it comes out into the open countryside of eastern Szechwan.

Eastern Szechwan is a low-lying plain, or basin, surrounded by high mountains. The Szechwan Basin is also known as the Red Basin because of the purplish-red color of its soil. The summer floods wash so much of this soil into the Yangtze that the soil stains the river a deep mahogany color.

At the port of Ipin, the river makes its last turn eastward. Here, for the first time, it becomes navigable for junks and steamboats. Also at Ipin, the Yangtze is joined by the Min River. Chengtu is located on the Min. To the people who live there, the Min is so important that they consider it the main river and the Yangtze its tributary.

On both sides of the Min, the rich red farmlands stretch to the horizon. But here and there, the basin is broken by terraced hills which have been sown with rice.

For the Szechwan farmer, the growing season is eleven months long. In the summer, the land is a glistening sea of young green rice. In the fall, the land is filled by the darker green of winter wheat. In the spring, everything is covered with the bright yellow flowers of the rape plant, which is grown for its oil.

Left: *A rice farmer labors in the fields during the growing season.*
Right: *Terraced fields stretch far to the horizon on both sides of the Min River.*

Clouds of bees hover over the fragrant rape flowers. They buzz in and out of hives which are arranged in orderly rows in the villages. Groves of mulberry trees surround some of the villages. Here, women and children with baskets over their arms carefully gather the tenderest mulberry leaves. When they have filled their baskets, they hurry off to the old village temple, where rows of boxes swarm with silkworms.

Taking care of the silkworms is a daily chore for the villagers. When the worms first hatch, they are no longer

*Mulberry trees are raised for their leaves, which is the favorite food of the silkworm—from an old woodcut.*

than a grain of rice. They eat mulberry leaves, which have to be chopped up fine. But soon the worms can get along without having the leaves chopped. They are such enormous eaters they have to be fed eight or nine times a day.

After about four weeks, the silkworm stops eating and spins its cocoon. The cocoons are left for ten days so that the worm can turn into a chrysalis. Then the cocoons are dropped into hot water and left there for ten minutes to kill the chrysalis. Afterwards, they are fished out. Now begins the work of unwinding the silk strands from which the cocoons are made.

In the big silk mills of eastern China, this work is done by machine. But in the little villages along the Min, the women unwind the cocoons by hand and spin the thread on foot-operated spinning wheels. Then the raw silk is carted off to the local mills to be woven into cloth, much of which will be exported to the communist countries of East Europe.

On the way upstream, the quiet of the countryside is broken at the coal-mining town of Kienwei. Here, the red earth is torn and gashed. Machinery clanks, and workmen with pickaxes swarm in and out of gaping entrances in the ground. Over everything hangs a haze of gray coal dust. The coal mined here is shipped to factory towns on the Yangtze.

Upriver from Kienwei is the famous salt-mining town of Wutungkiao, surrounded by a forest of tall derricks. They look like oil derricks, but they are made of wood.

They have been standing there for centuries. They draw saltwater from wells sunk thousands of feet into the ground. When the water evaporates, it leaves behind the fine black salt for which Szechwan is noted.

Despite its color, the salt tastes like white salt. It is packed into bags to be sold in the cities and towns of Szechwan. Great bags of it also go down the highway by truck to Yunnan Province, which has little salt.

A short distance beyond the salt derricks is the little silk-manufacturing town of Loshan, with its tiled-roof houses mounting the riverbank in tiers.

Above Loshan, the Min enters the broad plain in which Chengtu stands. Here, the river is split into several branches, which fan out across the plain. Canals radiate from each branch and water the whole area. This clever canal system is the work of two engineers, Li Ping and his son Li Erh-lang, who lived more than two thousand years ago. But it works as well today as it did then.

The canal system makes the water too shallow for steamers, so all river cargo must now travel on barges. Everything else on the plain seems to be headed for Chengtu also. Freight trains rumble in from the east, the south, and the north. Traffic jams the great highway that comes to the city from Lhasa.

All kinds of vehicles move down that highway. The trucks rumble along, stacked high with rocks, sand, and lumber for construction sites; wool and leather goods from Lhasa; tea, wine, and tobacco from western Szechwan; and

*The railway that goes north from Chengtu crosses the towering Tsen Ling range on its way to Paoki in Shensi Province.*

bales of cotton and raw silk for the Chengtu textile mills.

China hasn't nearly enough factories to manufacture the trucks she needs to transport goods. There aren't many mules or horses in this part of China to do this work either, and it must be done by humans. Teams of eight men in harness haul big lumbering carts filled with grain, cotton, kegs of honey, or squealing pigs. Farmers push squeaking, whining wheelbarrows heaped with fruits and vegetables from the outlying orchards and gardens. Processions of porters, stooped under their heavy loads, trudge along the edge of the highway.

Quite a number of people travel on shiny red bicycles. Others jam into old ramshackle buses. With horns blowing, the buses wheeze and clatter down the middle of the road. Most of the people are going to the city for a day of sightseeing. A lot of them are wearing necklaces of yellow jasmine. Jasmine grows everywhere in Szechwan Province, and anyone who wishes can make a necklace of it. But the necklaces aren't worn for ornamentation. The Szechwanese like the taste of this fragrant flower in their tea. When they order a cup of tea in one of the many teahouses in Chengtu, they strip off a few petals and drop them into the brew.

Everybody in China drinks tea. But no one considers tea just something you take with a meal. It is a ceremony of friendship. The first thing a guest is given when he enters a home is a cup of tea. This shows that he is welcome. And the little teahouses are just as particular as the people at home about greeting their patrons with a cup of tea as soon as they are seated.

From Chengtu, it is possible to return to the Yangtze by another water route. The canals that crisscross the plain are linked to a second tributary of that big river. This tributary is the To Kiang, a river that is much shallower than the Min. For most of the journey south, only rafts and small boats can navigate it.

On its way, the To Kiang flows through orchards of glossy-leafed orange trees and fields of soybeans and cotton. The soybean crops are processed into delicious bean curd, fine cooking oil, bean cakes which are used for cattle feed or fertilizer, and, of course, soy sauce. Most of these products are shipped to the big cities or farms of China but some are exported to Southeast Asia and Africa.

Left: *Orchards of orange trees grow in the countryside near the river.* Right: *Stacks of soybean cakes await shipment to the big cities or farms of China.*

The cotton is taken by barge to the textile mills of Chengtu, where it is woven into cloth. Then the finished product is shipped to towns and cities in Szechwan Province. Some of it goes by highway to Lhasa, the capital of Tibet, in the west, some to Yunnan Province. The cloth with the gayest designs goes to the Minority Peoples in the mountains, especially the little Miaos.

As the To Kiang flows south, it enters sugarcane country. Rows of tall-plumed sugarcane line its banks, extending across the valley and up the rolling hills beyond. Children and adults along the way are all chewing on pieces of sugarcane stalk as if it were candy. When the sugarcane is harvested, bundles of it are on the move everywhere. Buffaloes pull heavy carts stacked high with it. Porters carry great bundles of it fastened to their shoulder poles. Rafts going downstream are heaped with it. The sugarcane is headed for the sugar mill towns of Tzechung and Neikiang.

At the river port of Luchow, the To Kiang enters the Yangtze. There is always a cluster of barges and junks and perhaps even a small freighter or two drawn up here, taking on cargo. Porters swarm over the wharves and in and out of ships' holds, carrying heavy loads of sugar and salt, kegs of soy oil, large bean cakes, and baskets of oranges. This cargo is bound for cities and villages downstream.

## CHAPTER 5

# THE GORGE MOUNTAINS

The Yangtze rushes past Luchow and its wharves full of junks and riverboats. On the sloping green shores beyond Luchow, row after row of newly manufactured parasols have been spread out to dry. Made of brightly colored paper in gay shades of green, blue, red, pink, and yellow, the parasols gleam in the sun.

Pig-tailed girls scurry among the rows, gathering in the finished parasols and replacing them with wet ones. They will be sold in shops throughout Szechwan. Parasols are very popular with the Red Basin people, who use them to keep off the tropical sunshine as well as the torrential rains.

With every mile eastward, the countryside becomes more rugged. Finally, the river enters the Gorge Mountains, the last mountains it will have to pass through before it reaches the Middle Yangtze plains.

At the entrance to the Gorge Mountains is Chungking, the largest city in Szechwan Province and the most important transportation center in Southwest China. Trains from the south, the west, and the north all meet at Chungking. The river connects it to the great port of Shanghai at the mouth of the Yangtze. Highways join the city to the countryside. And twenty miles outside the city, there is an airfield where you can catch a plane for Peking.

The ancient city of Chungking crowns a rocky cliff and spills down its almost-sheer face. Two hundred feet above the water, bamboo shanties supported on rickety stilts hang over the river. Above the shanties, a jumble of houses climb the steep slopes in tiers.

Long flights of stairs lead up the cliff to the city. Most of the supplies needed by Chungking have to be carried up these steps by porters. The baskets that swing from their shoulders are heaped with vegetables, with sacks of grain and squawking geese, with fish, tea, and tobacco.

At the top of the cliff where the land levels off, the streets have been widened. Here there is a two-story, modern hotel, and below it, a big assembly building known as People's Hall. There are also blocks of modern apartment buildings. They aren't well-built, but they are much better than anything the people of Chungking had in earlier days. Then almost the entire city was a maze of filthy alleyways lined with hovels.

*Porters carry water and supplies in baskets up the long flight of stairs that lead to Chungking.*

But the poverty-stricken people of Chungking suffered even more in 1938. At that time, Chiang Kaishek, who governed China, made the city his wartime capital. The city was subjected to continual bombing raids by the Japanese. Many parts of it were destroyed and thousands of people died.

When peace finally came, the people of Chungking cooperated to rebuild their city. They formed street committees and waged war on the rats and flies that were causing epidemics of bubonic plague and cholera. Work brigades cleaned up the slimy alleyways and scoured and repaired the stone steps.

The street committees still operate in Chungking, as they do in every city on mainland China today. Each section of the city has its own street committee, made up of volunteer members. Besides seeing that things are kept clean, the committee helps settle quarrels. It conducts a clinic for the sick people in its neighborhood and runs nurseries for the children of working mothers. And it checks to be sure that everyone is loyal to the government in Peking.

There is more to Chungking than the city on the cliff. In the suburbs behind it, there are clusters of factories. Some

*Before the formation of street committees, slimy alleyways and run-down buildings bred rats and flies that caused epidemics.*

*Iron and steel works often use ore from nearby mines.*

manufacture farm implements and tools. Others make plastic goods. Textile mills weave cotton and silk. The iron and steel plant which Chiang Kaishek moved here during the war with Japan is now one of the nation's chief rail producers. It gets its iron ore from nearby mines.

There is plenty of coal in the vicinity too, which enables all the factories to operate full-time. But since many of them are equipped with outdated machinery, much of the work has to be done by hand-operated tools. It takes longer this way, and many more people are required to do the job.

45

Although the Chinese haven't the money to buy new machinery just now, the one thing they do have is a large labor force.

Chungking has suburbs on the far shores of both the Kialing and Yangtze rivers. These suburbs are run by farmers who work hard to reclaim the hillsides of their broken land. They have to grow as much food as possible for the people of Chungking.

A modern bridge crosses the Yangtze to the suburb on its southern shore. Trucks carry supplies to the city over this bridge. But the bridge cannot take all the traffic, so swarms of ferryboats dart back and forth, transporting goods and passengers.

The life of the people who live and work on the river is entirely different from that of the city folk. Their homes are in the jumble of houseboats and junks which are drawn up at the foot of the great bluff on which Chungking stands.

Junks are flat-bottomed boats with high sterns, square bows, and sails of bamboo matting. There are junks of all sizes in China. Every river has its own style of junk and shape of sail. The junks are used for fishing, for carrying cargo, and as homes for the people who own them.

Entire families sleep crowded together in narrow boxlike compartments in the hold of the junks. But most of their time is spent on deck. The women wash clothes in the river water. At mealtime, with trousers rolled to their knees, they cook rice and vegetables and a little bit of fish on charcoal braziers. The deck is the children's only playground. They are trained early to be careful, and few fall overboard.

The junks that make the dangerous run through the Gorge Mountains from Chungking to the Middle Yangtze Plain are stout, chunky boats, and their crews are especially skillful. They have to know where the dangerous reefs are and be ready with their grappling hooks to shove away from the steep canyon walls. They have to have muscular arms to row against the current. And they have to know how to set their sails to catch the favorable breezes.

Their hardest work comes when they have to go upstream against the current and there is no wind to help them. Then they attach a strong rope to the boat and, bent

*The junk sailing on the Yangtze River is used for carrying cargo, fishing, and as a home for its owners.*

double against the force of the current, they trudge along the narrow towpath at the water's edge, hauling their junk after them. Towing a boat in this way is called tracking, and the men are called trackers.

Junks line the Chungking waterfront to take on cargo. Processions of porters bring loads of silk and cotton, plastic goods, rice, vegetables, and sugar. As soon as the hold is filled, the junk men cast off and start their run downstream.

Beyond Chungking, the Yangtze cuts a corridor between steep brush-covered hills and high mountain slopes. Along this stretch, it is known as the Great River.

Freighters and small passenger ships keep the junks company on the winding river. The boats stop at river ports along the way to unload cargoes of salt and cotton for the people of the mountains, and to take on gall nuts, tung oil, and medicinal herbs for the cities of the plain.

The steamboats going downstream need two days to get through the Gorge Mountains. On the second day, they make one of the most scenic trips in the world. It is the run through the one hundred and thirty mile stretch of river known as the Three Gorges.

The first of the gorges is called the Wind Box. Here, the river rushes between cliffs that rise three to four thousand feet high. Little houses of stone or bamboo cling to the face of the cliffs. The people who live there are fishermen. Perching on rocks just above the waterline, they dip up fish with long, narrow butterfly-type nets.

Below the Wind Box is the Wuhsia Gorge. Wuhsia

means Magician Wu, and the gorge is named after Wu Hsien, the famous magician of the Shang Dynasty who ruled China from 1600 to 1028 B.C.

Peaks a mile high tower above the Wuhsia Gorge. One of the peaks is shaped like a graceful woman. Legend says she is a goddess who loved the river people so much that she sent heavenly birds to guide them through her canyon.

The worst rapids of all lie in this gorge. In the old days, it took three hundred trackers to haul one junk up the

*Sheer cliffs line one of the gorges of the Yangtze River.*

Wuhsia rapids. The trackers had to trudge along narrow towpaths cut in the cliff walls more than a hundred feet above the river. Sometimes they would slip off the narrow trail to their deaths. Sometimes the boat would be caught in a giant whirlpool and swallowed instantly.

Now a deep channel has been blasted through the rapids, and a chain of lighted buoys makes it possible for ships to travel even at night. But this stretch is still very dangerous, especially when the river is swollen by summer rains and the melting snows of Tibet.

Then, in a very short while, the water may rise as much as two hundred and fifty feet. The rapids are swallowed by a rush of giant red waves and spinning whirlpools. At such times, only the captains of the biggest steamships dare to go through Wuhsia Gorge.

The last of the gorges is called the Gorge of the Western Grave. It is seventy-five miles long. Gray limestone cliffs and wierd red sandstone formations carved by wind and rain line the water. In steep wooded ravines, the ruins of old temples and crumbling pagodas stand forlornly. Many pilgrims used to come there to pray to the river god for safe passage on the Yangtze. Now they are seldom visited by anyone.

## CHAPTER 6

# THE MIDDLE PLAINS

Beyond the village of Ichang, below the Gorge of the Western Grave, the Yangtze rolls through its last canyon, the Tiger's Tooth Gorge, and comes out into flat country-side. This is known as the Middle Yangtze Plain. It stretches away for miles, broken here and there by little knots of hills. Glistening lakes line the Yangtze every-where. Many of the lakes are natural ones. Others are man-made reservoirs.

Canals crisscross the country, stringing the lakes to-gether. The peasants like to call their canals "vines" and their lakes "melons." They will tell you "Our vines are heavy with melons."

Occasional snow flurries visit the plain in the winter,

*Taken at Ichang, this picture shows heavily-loaded junks as they approach Wu-San Gorge. In order to navigate the more dangerous parts of the river, coolies on the shore had to pull the boats with long bamboo cables.*

but the climate is generally quite mild. Spring comes early, and then the farmers begin to prepare seed beds for the rice.

The seed beds are small oblongs of land enclosed in dikes. The beds are sowed, and flooded. By the time the sprouts stand two or three inches high, the winter wheat, which was planted the fall before, is ready for harvesting. It has to be done in a hurry. But the peasants have lots of help from the city.

Everyone in Communist China is supposed to spend some time each year helping out on the farms. Factory workers, professors, students, engineers, technicians, and ballet troupes all go to the fields to do their share. There are even companies of soldiers and their officers in khaki coats and caps. Most of the soldiers are from the country and know all about farming. So they are very efficient at mowing down the wheat with their long scythes, binding it into sheaves, and threshing it.

As soon as the wheat is harvested, the fields are plowed in preparation for the rice. Much of the plowing is done with buffaloes, since there are not enough tractors. Afterwards, water is let into the fields from the canals and lakes.

Then men, women, and companies of young soldiers wade through the mud with baskets of young seedlings over their arms. They rise and stoop, rise and stoop, as they set out the tiny plants, one by one, in neat rows. By midsummer a sea of green rice ripples in the breeze.

Rice needs a lot of water. Though about fifty inches of rain fall on the Central Yangtze Plain every year, irrigation is still necessary. Electric pumps along the river and the large canals siphon the water into pipes which lead to the fields.

Old-fashioned waterwheels and treadles are at work too. They are each run by two persons, one on either side, pedaling away.

During this part of its course, the Yangtze makes many turns, and its width changes frequently. It is stained so red by the silt it carries that the Chinese sometimes call it the River of Copper.

*Three women sow rice in flooded seed beds enclosed by dikes.*

*When there are no tractors, the plowing is done with buffaloes.*

Life along the riverbank is varied. At a boatyard, men in blue trousers and jackets fill the air with the sound of sawing and hammering. On one side, a row of kilns lines the bank. And down at the river's edge, men and women busily dig out wet clay which they will turn into bricks and bake in the kilns. Stacks of newly manufactured gray bricks stand along the riverbank, waiting to be transported in barges to building sites on the river. Farther along, a team of workers perch on a flimsy wooden scaffolding, twisting long thick strands of bamboo fibre together to make stout ropes for tracking. In the shade of elm and willow trees, women weave nylon fishing nets. Some of the nets will be used by the river fishermen, but most of them will be exported to far-away Uganda or to other African countries. Occasionally, the buzz of electric drills and saws drifts out of a riverside village where farm tools are being manufactured by modern methods.

Through the centuries, the Yangtze has not been kind to the people who live along its banks. During particularly heavy rainfalls, the river has often risen high enough to sweep away villages and flood the farmlands. One of the worst of these floods occurred in 1931, when seven cyclones passed over the plain one after the other. Water poured down in sheets, filling the river until it burst from its banks to cover thirty-four thousand square miles of farmland. Only the tops of trees showed that this expanse of water had once been solid earth. One hundred and forty thousand people were drowned. Ten to twenty-five million were made homeless, and many starved to death.

Above: *During 1931 when seven cyclones passed over the Yangtze plains, villages and farmlands were severely flooded.*
Below: *With pickaxes, shovels, baskets, and wheelbarrows, these peasants who live along the flooded river are reclaiming their land.*

In 1954, an even worse flood occurred. Then the water covered more than forty-one thousand square miles, which is ten percent of all the farmland in China. Ten million people had to be evacuated. But, by this time, the government was well-organized. Help came quickly, so there was very little loss of life.

After the 1954 flood, more than three hundred thousand peasants who lived along the river dug a flood-retention basin. This is a large basin into which the river waters can be turned in times of flood. Their only tools were pickaxes, shovels, baskets, and wheelbarrows. With these tools they hollowed out a basin that covered more than three hundred and fifty square miles. A dam and sluice gates were installed to connect the new basin with the Yangtze River. Today it is known as Kingkiang Basin.

East of Kingkiang Basin, the Yangtze soon comes to the mouth of another basin. This one was made by nature. It is Tungting Lake, the second-largest natural freshwater lake in China.

Below Tungting Lake are the South Yangtze Hills. Their northern slopes form the watershed of the Yangtze. Three large rivers and many smaller ones come through the mountains and empty into Tungting Lake. If it were not for this lake, they would all flood into the Yangtze.

The largest of the three rivers is the Siang Kiang. Changsha, the capital of Hunan Province, is located on this river. Trains from Peking to the north and Canton to the south stop at Changsha. But it is still a typical old-style

*In a shop in Changsha, a stocking maker takes an hour to finish one stocking.*

*A reading room in the workers' club at a Changsha rubber-boot factory.*

Chinese city. It has winding lanes, hemmed in by the gray walls of tile-roofed houses. Its greatest claim to fame is that Mao Tsetung, who has been Chairman of the Chinese Communist Party, since 1949 was born nearby.

Chairman Mao was born in the little mountain community of Shao Shan. Visitors from all over the country come to visit it, because Mao Tsetung is still the most revered man on mainland China.

Though Mao became the hero of the poverty-stricken peasants of China, his family were well-to-do farmers. Their comfortable fourteen-room farmhouse stands on the side of a wooded hill.

Some three thousand farmers live in the Shao Shan area. All of them belong to Mao Tsetung's clan, and they have the surname Mao too. They are very proud to share their name and their past with him. They welcome all visitors and enjoy showing them Mao's boyhood home.

## CHAPTER 7

# MIGHTY WUHAN

The upland valleys of the South Yangtze Hills have just the right climate and amount of moisture for cultivating tea. And here there are plantations of low, glossy-leafed tea bushes growing in orderly rows.

The bushes never get any larger because they are kept pruned to this size to make picking easy. In early April, when the new growth begins to appear, women with baskets over their arms strip off the young leaves. They work quickly because they have learned how to do the job by using both hands.

At night, other workers roast the tea leaves in pans over low fires. They have to keep turning the leaves so they won't scorch. After about forty minutes, the leaves are properly toasted and shriveled. This process is known as curing the tea. Afterwards, the leaves are packed and sent down to the big cities. Much of the tea will be used by the Chinese themselves. The rest will be exported to countries in Southeast Asia, Europe, and Africa.

On the mountain slopes high above the tea plantations, rain falls so abundantly that the forests grow thick and

*Rain forests of the South Yangtze Hills are thick with trees.*

fast. The rain forests of the South Yangtze Hills are made up of fir, pine, cypress, and bamboo.

Lumber camps are in operation here. The men who run them make sure they will always have forests by planting a new tree for each one they cut down.

The felled trees are sawed into logs which are hauled to the rivers. There they are fastened together to form rafts, some of which are an acre in size. Then the raft men and their families take over. They build a thatched hut in the center of each raft. This will be their home until the lumber is delivered.

Finally the journey begins. The men use long poles to push the rafts down river. Occasionally, they stop to pick up cargoes of cotton, rice, and tea. Presently they leave the rivers behind, cross Tungting Lake, and enter the Yangtze itself. They are headed downstream for Wuhan, one of China's largest industrial and transportation centers.

When the rafts reach Wuhan, the men bring them in to shore and transfer the thatched huts to the riverbank. Here the families live till the cargo has been disposed of and the rafts have been broken apart. The logs will be carted off to lumber mills to be sawed into planks for use in building houses or making furniture. The families return to the high mountains by junk or barge to steer down another log raft. This is the daily routine of the raft folk.

In the turbulent red Yangtze, the rafts join other traffic, barges, cargo junks, and freighters, all rushing to Wuhan. It is really a triple city, standing at the juncture of the

Yangtze and her most important tributary, the Han River.

The three cities of Wuhan are Wuchang, Hanyang, and Hankow. First comes Wuchang, oldest of the three, on the south bank of the Yangtze. Its waterfront is lined with railroad repair shops and shipyards. The ancient part of Wuchang stands on hilly ground behind old walls. Here the administrative buildings and a government mint are situated.

The modern buildings of the University of Wuhan

*More than 5,000 swimmers in Wuhan followed Chairman Mao Tsetung into the waters of the Yangtze River. They were taking part in the eleventh cross-Yangtze swimming competition.*

sprawl over the hills among pleasant woods. The large complex includes an agricultural college, a teachers' college, and many engineering colleges. In recent years, a new medical college and several hospitals have been added. More than three thousand young medical students are training to be doctors.

A modern double-decker bridge across the river connects Wuchang with Hanyang. It was built with Russian help and was completed in 1958. Almost a mile long, the bridge is so high that even when the river floods, ships of several thousand tons can clear it easily. A steady stream of buses, pedestrians, and bicycles stream over the top deck. Long passenger and freight trains rumble through the lower one.

As the Yangtze passes under the bridge, the choppy waters of the Han flow into it from the north. Hanyang is on the right bank of the Han. Hankow, which is on the left bank of the Han, also sprawls along the northern shore of the Yangtze.

Hankow is the largest of the three cities. Junks, tug-

*The Yangtze Bridge at Wuhan is a modern double-decker bridge built with Russian help.*

boats, barges, and freighters constantly surround its wharves. When the river is in flood, ocean-going steamboats can come as far inland as Hankow. The wharves are the first really modern ones on the Yangtze so far. Stevedores operate the cranes and inclined hoists that do the loading and unloading. Later, trucks and thousands of porters carry the stacked goods and materials to warehouses or construction sites.

Hankow was developed by British, French, and American businessmen. They began settling there in 1861. They built large homes, ten-story warehouses, and office buildings along the waterfront.

Today, the foreigners have gone, and the buildings are occupied by Chinese. One of the largest buildings has been transformed into an amusement center. Such amusement centers have been established in all the big cities of China. They are called Cultural Palaces, and they are run by the labor unions, which are controlled by the government in Peking.

Everything in the amusement center is free. There is a gymnasium where one can exercise or play games. There are puppet shows and reading rooms lined with communist magazines and books. Classes are given in reading and writing, in drawing and acting, and in singing or playing musicial instruments. At night, the students perform concerts or Chinese operas in the auditoriums of the amusement center. Often, after dark, the sound of fiddles and cymbals or singing drifts out over the Yangtze from the brightly lighted Cultural Palace in Hankow.

*This iron and steel works employs thousands of people.*

Hankow has changed through the years. Many of its narrow winding lanes have been widened into streets. The old hovels have given way to rows of apartment buildings.

Though the streets are wide, one sees few cars on them but numerous bicycles. And there are three hundred and fifty modern buses which are always crammed with people going somewhere.

Some of the buses cross to Hanyang by a bridge that spans the Han River. These buses are jammed with workers. Down a wide hardtop road flanked by a railway, the buses roll. Finally, they draw up before a gigantic iron and steel works to let their passengers off.

The iron and steel works covers six square miles of what was once farmland on the outskirts of Hanyang. Now it is a bustling industrial center, where thousands of people are employed.

Rich beds of coal in the vicinity provide fuel for the works. Iron ore is brought from nearby mines by an electric train. The ore is smelted by great blast furnaces and transformed into ingots. These ingots will be carted off to the factories of Wuhan to make farm implements and heavy machinery.

Scattered among the workmen are women in their twenties, dressed in white smocks, their long black braids gathered up under cotton caps. Some of them are operating the overhead machinery that carries glowing ingots across

*Throughout China today, women handle machinery and do jobs that were once forbidden to them by China's ancient traditions.*

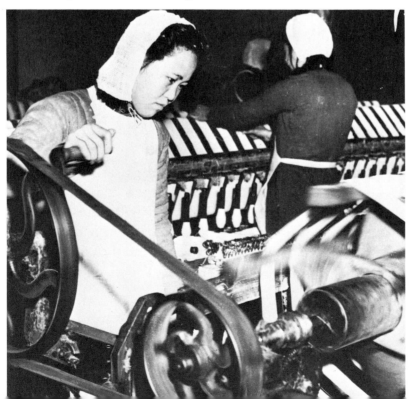

the huge workshops to drop them gently on rollers. Other young women are serving as technicians and electricians.

Before the communists came to power in China, the women were never allowed to work with machinery. They were expected to stay at home, and few of them received an education. Today, girls and boys get equal schooling. And the girls are just as eager as the boys to become engineers, drive tractors or buses, or operate cranes.

The Wuhan iron and steel works was established in 1955, when forty-five Russian experts came to advise the Chinese on how to construct such a center. At that time, Russia, which is also a communist nation, was very friendly with China.

Then Russia and China started to quarrel. Each nation began to accuse the other of not being a good communist country. In communist countries, everything is owned and controlled by the government. The government sets the prices on farm products. It owns the factories and pays wages to the workers. On the other hand, in countries like the United States, England, and France, land and businesses are owned by private individuals who fix the prices and pay the wages. The Communists call such countries "capitalist" nations.

Much of the quarrel between Russia and China was about these "capitalist" nations. China complained that Russia was beginning to make friends with these nations, instead of treating them like enemies as a true communist country should. She accused Russia herself of turning into a capitalist nation because she had begun paying people bonuses when they turned out more work. China said true communists should do the extra work for nothing.

Russia said that China's kind of communism was old-fashioned. Instead of fighting capitalist nations, communists could live at peace with them and still win people over to communism. She said that China was splitting the communist nations by her public criticisms.

By 1960, the quarrel had gotten so bitter that Russia pulled all her technicians out of China. They even took their blueprints along, leaving the Wuhan iron and steel works uncompleted. The Chinese engineers had to work slowly. Studying textbooks, they carried out experiments and made costly mistakes before they finished the giant complex.

Today, the ill will between China and Russia is still present. This has led to trouble along their mutual boundaries. The people of Wuhan feel particularly bitter because they believe the Russians have betrayed them.

Wuhan contains many other industries besides the iron and steel works: textile and paper mills, chemical and cement plants, a heavy machine-tool factory, and other factories which make farm implements. There is also a large meat-packing plant, where pigs are processed for export to countries in East Europe.

Like most modern industrial centers, Wuhan is a smoky, grimy city. But it is surrounded with pleasant parks and lakes. On Sundays, the parks are alive with gaily dressed people enjoying family picnics. Sunday is the only day Communist Chinese workers get off.

## CHAPTER 8

# THE WATER COUNTRY

Beyond Wuhan, the Yangtze receives the waters of another lake. It is called Poyang, and it is the largest natural fresh water lake in China. At last, the river enters the region where it has always been known as the Yangtze. In 2000 B.C., this region was part of Yang Province, and that is where the river's name came from.

By this time, the Yangtze has traveled some thirty-four hundred miles from its source in the Tibetan-Chinghai plateau, and it has only two hundred miles to go before it reaches the Pacific. The lively market town of Wuhu stands at this point. Beyond it, the land is so flat that the sea tides come all the way upriver to the town.

This stretch of the Yangtze is very important historically to the Communist Chinese because it is the scene of the last important battle of their civil war. In April of 1949, the Nationalist troops were lined up along the south bank of the river, the Communist troops along the north. With the Yangtze as their defense line, the Nationalist army was sure it was safe.

But the peasants, who were still on the side of the Communists, gathered together all their skiffs and fishing boats. Soon, hundreds of them were hidden away in the marshes north of the river. One dark night, with the peasants acting as oarsmen, the Communists launched their flimsy flotilla.

Despite strafing from Nationalist machine guns, the little boats kept coming. By the twenty-first of April, the Communists had made a full-scale landing all along the riverfront. Two days later, the Nationalists' capital, Nanking, fell.

The crossing of the river was the end for the Nationalist forces. Before the year was out, they had retreated to the

*Mao Tsetung and Chiang Kaishek toast each other at a truce conference arranged in 1945.*

island of Formosa, or Taiwan. Today, Chiang Kaishek rules Taiwan, while the communists control the Chinese mainland.

Nanking stands on the south bank of the river on the site of an ancient town built in the second century B.C. Since then, the city has been destroyed again and again by wars and rebellions. Today it is more modern than most cities in China. The young people of the city are especially proud of their university, the University of Nanking, with its new scientific-research complex.

But Nanking also still has a few historical spots. The famous tombs and great stone animals of the Ming Dynasty can be found in the Eastern Hills, which rise behind the city. And on the slopes of Purple Mountain is the mausoleum of Sun Yat-sen, Father of the Chinese Revolution, who died in 1925.

Fifty miles downstream from Nanking, the river reaches the busy port of Chinkiang. Here, a steady procession of cargo junks and barges move north and south from Chinkiang through a wide canal. This is the famous Grand Canal, which stretches from Hangchow in the south to Peking more than a thousand miles away to the north. Over the years, many Chinese emperors lengthened the canal, which was needed to transport grain to their courts.

The Yangtze has now entered the low-lying delta region, the famous Water Country. Green paddy-fields are thickly webbed with canals and ponds. More canals and ponds are found here than in any other place in China.

*In the Eastern Hills behind Nanking are the famous tombs and great stone statues of the Ming Dynasty.*

The Chinese call the delta the Land of Fish and Rice. Everything yields food. Along the edges of the ponds, men and women harvest water chestnuts or gather the roots of the fragrant pink lotus-lily, which make good eating.

In the canals, fishermen on skiffs are cormorant fishing. These big black birds have had their wings clipped so that they are unable to fly away. Each one wears a tight collar around its long neck. From the rim of its master's skiff, the cormorant stares down into the water. When it spies a fish, it dives off, makes its catch, and returns to the skiff to eat the fish. But it can't swallow the fish because the collar is too tight. The fisherman takes the fish away and puts it into his basket, and the cormorant starts looking for another.

73

The air along the riverbank is filled with the rank odor of decaying material. The odor comes from a row of circular-shaped compost pits, which are used to make natural fertilizer. The Chinese need many thousands of such pits because they haven't enough modern plants to manufacture the fertilizer needed for all their fields. Even the children help out. They gather droppings from pig sties, chicken coops, and grazing grounds to bring to the compost pits.

All the children in the farm communities do their share of the work. Some of them wade knee-deep in the muddy paddy-fields, trying to scoop up fish for an evening meal with their butterfly nets. The Chinese breed fish in their fields. The fish not only provide food, but they also help by eating destructive pests and fertilizing the young plants with their droppings.

*Fishermen use cormorants to catch fish.*

*In farm communities, all children—no matter how small—must do their share of work.*

Other children work waterwheels or weed. Small children herd flocks of indignant geese by waving long sticks with tassles at the end. In the early morning, older children ride lumbering water buffaloes out to the pasture lands. They will stay with the animals all day and bring them home at night. There are many buffaloes in this part of China. They are treated with great care because they are needed to help with the plowing.

Most of the farm communities have small schoolhouses where the children can go at least for part-time study. In the poorer villages, these schoolhouses are little mud-brick buildings put up by the peasants. Even the desks are made of dried mud.

Communist Chinese schools do not give marks to individual pupils. Instead, the class is graded as a whole.

Better students stay after school to help the poorer ones. Everyone wants to bring up the standing of his class.

Schools in farm communities are no longer run by communist officials from Peking, as they once were. The peasants themselves form the school board, and most of the teachers are teen-agers. This change was made in August of 1966, after Mao Tsetung launched the Cultural Revolution.

*Throughout China, posters showing Mao with groups of children are designed "to deepen their love" for Mao and his communist teachings.*

Mao Tsetung started the movement when he began to feel that the Chinese were falling away from true communism. He had found out that some of the Communist Party officials who had been sent from Peking to advise the farm communities were treating the peasants like serfs.

In the cities, he had discovered that some factories were paying bonuses to workers, just as was being done in Russia. Worst of all, to Mao's thinking, communist officials such as Liu Shaochi, President of the Party, were openly endorsing the Russian kind of communism. Mao Tsetung felt he had to break the power of these men.

He was also worried about the young people of China. They had never known hardships like those their parents and grandparents had experienced before the communist take-over. He was afraid that when they grew up they would prefer a soft life and would let communism die in China. So Mao sponsored an organization for school children called the Red Guard. The children were given little red books called *The Sayings of Mao Tsetung*. The books contained selections from Mao Tsetung's works, written during the early days of communism in China. The children read and reread these sayings and discussed them until they knew them by heart.

In 1966, when the Cultural Revolution began, the schools were closed, and all over China the children of the Red Guard took to the road. Most of them were teenagers, but some were as young as eight. They traveled in bands, from district to district and province to province.

Sometimes they walked, sometimes they rode without paying on buses and trains. Wherever they went, they took along their little red books.

The Red Guard was given the power to investigate peasants in the country and factory workers in the cities to see if they were following Mao Tsetung's thoughts. The peasants called the Red Guard "the little generals."

After two years, the Cultural Revolution was brought to an end, and the Red Guard was disbanded. Then the teen-agers were told that people had to make sacrifices in a revolution. Their sacrifice was to give up all thought of further education for themselves. Instead, they were to spend the rest of their lives in farm communities, living and working with the peasants.

Some of the teen-agers didn't like this, but most of them went cheerfully because they had been taught that this was all part of a revolution. After all, when the heroes of the Long March had won their revolution, they too had gone out to work among the people.

*At Mao's old school in Hunan Province, fighters of the Red Second Company and young Red Guards talk about* The Sayings of Mao Tsetung.

## CHAPTER 9

# DOWN TO THE SEA

As the Yangtze nears the ocean, it flows through very sandy and salty soil. Cotton grows well in this kind of earth, so broad fields of cotton stretch away northward.

A good cotton crop does not happen easily. Sometimes hordes of insects descend on the bushes. China has very little in the way of insecticides to take care of such emergencies. Therefore, the peasants fight the insects with the simple methods they have been using for centuries.

During an insect plague, every field is surrounded by a long line of big brown earthenware jars. These jars, filled with vinegar flavored with sugar, lure thousands of insects to their death. At night, flickering lamps dot the fields. The lamps are made from empty insecticide bottles filled with water. The lights attract the moths which fly blindly into the bottles of water.

Sometimes, instead of flying insects, pink bollworms attack the cotton. Then armies of children join the adults in searching the ripening bolls for these tiny destructive creatures, which they crush one by one.

When harvest time comes, it is a season of rejoicing. Then, as far as the eye can see, white cotton fluffs cover the bushes. Men, women, and children, with baskets over their arms, go through the fields to pick the snowy bolls.

The cotton is baled and shipped to the mills of Nantung, a large textile center which stands on the Yangtze about eighty-five miles below Chinkiang. There the cotton will be woven into high-grade cloth, much of it to be exported to countries in Southeast Asia and Africa.

Beyond Nantung, the Yangtze River begins to widen.

*At textile centers on the Yangtze River, cotton is woven into high grade cloth to be exported to other countries.*

This is its estuary, or mouth. The surface of the water is broken by long sandbars and small islands. They have been built up from the billions of cubic feet of silt the Yangtze brings downstream each year.

The estuary is too wide and is exposed to gales and the water is too shallow to provide a good harbor. So the ocean port of Shanghai had to be built on the little Hwang Pu River, which flows into the estuary from the south. Freighters, passenger steamers, and cargo junks all have to make their way fifteen miles upstream to dock at the Shanghai wharves.

Shanghai itself stands barely above sea level on tidal mud flats. Tall skyscrapers on the streets of the central business district line the west bank of the Hwang Pu. The skyscrapers rest on hundreds of piles which have been driven into the soft mud. They were designed by western architects and built with foreign money. Before World War II, these skyscrapers were the tallest buildings in the world except for those in the United States. They gave Shanghai the appearance of an American seaport.

Houses and factories sprawl out for miles around the business section. There are crowded suburbs east of the Hwang Pu and south of Soochow Creek, which flows into the Hwang Pu from the west.

Today, Shanghai covers more than three hundred and fifty square miles and is one of the largest cities in the world. Nobody knows how many people live there. The number ranges anywhere between ten and twelve million.

*Shanghai's streets are lined with tall skyscrapers that extend along the west bank of the Hwang Pu.*

Most of them work in fish canneries, food-processing plants, or factories. All kinds of things are being manufactured, from drugs and surgical instruments to trucks, fountain pens, and cameras. Many of these articles are not only sold in the big cities of China, but are also exported to Southeast Asia and Africa.

There is a petroleum refinery too, which is supplied with crude oil that is carried to Shanghai by rail from Yumen in faraway Kansu Province. A giant steel mill gets its iron ore from up the Yangtze.

Like Hankow, Shanghai was developed by foreigners. It was just a little fishing village and trading center in 1843, at which time the Chinese government permitted other nations to establish business houses and build homes there.

By 1888, the first modern factory in China had been built in Shanghai. It was a textile mill which used the raw silk provided by the silkworm farms from the surrounding countryside. By the 1930's, Shanghai had almost two thousand factories. They were owned by Chinese as well as foreigners. The foreign businessmen had found there was a high profit in manufacturing here, because labor was so cheap.

One of the chief sources of labor was young children. In times of famine, contractors would go out into the countryside or to city slums where families were starving and buy children. Then they would hire them out to the factory owners. The contractors provided boards for the children to sleep on. The factory owners gave them meager rations of food.

Boys and girls less than nine years old stood in long lines, over boiling vats filled with silkworm cocoons. The children had to keep the cocoons in the water and then

*Members of a drill team at a petroleum refinery study Mao's works during their break.*

take them out at the right time. They worked from six in the morning until six at night. Each year, hundreds died, but the contractors were always able to get more children to replace them.

Life wasn't much better for adults. They lived crowded together in slums, more than three hundred thousand people to a square mile. Their homes were shanties made of pieces of board fastened together, or discarded bamboo mattings, or old tin cans, or even newspapers. Many with no homes just slept in the open.

Today, children no longer slave in the silk mills. There are better living quarters for workers around some of the factories. Here, rows of apartment buildings stand on tree shaded streets. On the outside, the apartment buildings look like many in America. But inside, the narrow halls are unplastered and dimly lighted, and the concrete stairs are steep and uncarpeted.

The apartments themselves are tiny. The largest have two bedrooms, a cubbyhole toilet and shower, and a kitchen. A family of eight may all crowd together in one of these apartments.

There are still slums in Shanghai. And they will have to stay until enough housing can be built to take care of the millions of people who live in this city. Many of the slum-dwellers are untrained laborers. When work falls off, as it did during the unrest of the Cultural Revolution, they are the first to lose their jobs. There was a great deal of suffering in Shanghai at that time.

Trouble began when the Red Guard swarmed in, wav-

*The youthful Red Guard swarm through the streets carrying Mao's red books, a portrait of Karl Marx, and shouting slogans.*

ing their little red books, shouting slogans, and singing revolutionary songs. They began pasting posters on the walls.

Wall posters are a common thing in China. Many of them are official notices from the government. But any person can paste a poster on a public wall. All day long, crowds of curious people cluster round the posters, reading them.

The posters of the Red Guard proclaimed such things as "Down with Liu Shaochi!" "Down with Russian Communism!" "Down with traitors to Mao Tsetung."

After they put up their posters, the Red Guard marched to the factories. They criticized the workers for taking bonuses and the managers because they weren't acting like good communists. Soon the Red Guard had stirred up the city, and people began to take sides.

Some agreed with the Red Guard and Mao Tsetung. Those who did not want to give up their bonuses sided with Liu Shaochi. They too began to paste up posters. Their posters read "Down with the Red Guard!" "Don't interfere with our rights!" "Pigs of Red Guards get out of Shanghai!"

As feelings got higher and higher, little work was done in the factories, and street fights erupted. People dragged furniture out of the factories and stacked it in the streets

*All day long, crowds of curious people stop to read the posters pasted on the walls by the Red Guard.*

to make barricades. Using guns and clubs and knives, they fought from behind these barricades.

A number of people were killed before soldiers from the People's Liberation Army arrived to restore order.

The People's Liberation Army was kept busy in other big cities too in Wuhan and Nanking and Canton.

Finally, in 1968, the Cultural Revolution came to an end. Mao Tsetung had won the struggle, and Liu Shaochi had lost his power. This was because most of the people, especially the peasants, trusted Mao Tsetung. He had kept his promises to them. He had given them the land, and though life was still hard, it was much better than it had ever been before.

Even the quarrelsome workers in the big cities decided it was better to settle down to an orderly life again. Once more the factories opened in Shanghai.

From Shanghai, ocean-going freighters descend the Hwang Pu and turn eastward into the Yangtze estuary. Along the way, they pass shipyards and ice plants. Modern trawlers are drawn up in front of the plants, and long conveyor belts carry blocks of ice into the trawlers' holds. The ice preserves the fish, and allows the fishermen to spend several days at sea.

During this course of the journey, the ships need trained pilots to guide them through the tricky man-made channel. In order to keep the channel open, some three million tons of silt has to be removed each year.

The most treacherous spot of all is where the Yangtze

enters the sea. There, the way is blocked by a series of huge sandbars. The Chinese call them the Fairy Flats. The water surrounding the Fairy Flats is less than twenty feet deep at low tide. Large freighters have to wait for the fifteen-foot-high incoming tide to carry them safely through.

Beyond the Fairy Flats, the Yangtze is left behind, but not its silt. The warm Japan Current, which flows along the coast of China, carries silt seventy-five miles south to the Chu Shan Islands. The islands lie in the world-famous Chu Shan fishing grounds and are inhabited solely by fishermen.

In the winter, the fishermen catch hairtails, and in the summer big yellow croakers. They also bring in tons of cuttlefish. In the summertime, the island hillsides and even the tile roofs of the village houses are covered with strong-smelling fish laid out in the sun to dry. Then they are shipped to the mainland for sale to the people in big cities.

The Chu Shan Islands won't always be separated from the coast of China. The millions of tons of silt which the Japan Current drops here yearly will one day turn them into a rocky promontory knitted to the mainland by the red soil of the Yangtze.

## CHAPTER 10

# PLANS FOR THE YANGTZE

Almost two hundred and thirty million people live in the basin of the Yangtze. This is about a third of China's population and one tenth of all the people in the world. They all depend on the river for their survival.

People in other parts of China depend on the Yangtze too. It is the country's greatest transportation system. It would take two hundred railroads running parallel to it to move the cargoes that it carries so easily.

The Chinese have many plans for their great river. One plan is to connect the Yangtze to the Yellow River by way of the Han. Another plan is to divert some of the Yangtze headwaters north by canal to the Taklamakan Desert so that the desert can be cultivated.

The biggest plan of all is to build a dam at the foot of

the Three Gorges. This would change the rushing river into a lake and allow ocean-going freighters to travel as far as Chungking.

Many obstacles will have to be overcome before these plans come true. Perhaps they will never be accomplished. But other plans are coming true each year.

To make transportation easier, the banks of the Yangtze are being spanned with more and more bridges. One of the longest of these is the one recently completed at Nanking, which was built without any foreign aid.

Dams and hydroelectric plants are going up on numerous Yangtze tributaries. They provide electricity for irrigation pumps as well as for new factories and villages and towns which before had only kerosene lamps.

The peasants themselves are helping in the work by digging additional flood retention basins along the banks of the Yangtze and its tributaries. They are cutting long

*Dams and hydroelectric plants like this one are being built on many tributaries of the Yangtze.*

trunk lines from the basins to the surrounding countryside. Smaller canals from the trunk lines spread a web of water over the once arid land.

It is backbreaking work because the trunk lines have to be kept level. Sometimes the peasants have to hack their way through hills, and at other times they have to fill up valleys. Their only tools are hoes and pickaxes and an occasional bulldozer or two. But nothing stops them.

In the hilly country, they make use of the hills themselves. They even dig shallow reservoirs on the summits and cut terraces into the slopes of the hills. Then they lay pipes from the canal below to the reservoir above. They call the pipes "water dragons."

On the canal banks, electric pumps send water shooting up the pipes to fill the reservoirs. When the terraced fields need water, irrigation ditches lead the water back down again. Irrigation means that even during "droughts fierce as tigers" the fields on the hills stay green.

But the canals and reservoirs serve the peasants in other ways too. They are all stocked with fish and shrimp. Water chestnuts and lotus plants are cultivated around the edges of canals and reservoirs. The water-weeds which grow in them are gathered to fertilize the fields. In China, no chance of providing extra food is ever lost.

Every year, new canals carry the life-giving waters of the Yangtze deeper and deeper into the countryside. Bit by bit, the peasants are forcing their majestic river to help them in the work of feeding the hungry millions of China.

# PRONUNCIATION GUIDE

| WORD | PRONUNCIATION | WORD | PRONUNCIATION |
|---|---|---|---|
| **Bayan Kara** | Bah-yahn-kah-rah | **Li Ping** | Lee Bing |
| **Canton** | Cahn-tahn | **Lisu** | Lee-soo |
| **Changsha** | Chahng-shah | **Liu Shaochi** | Lee-oo Shao-chee |
| **Chengtu** | Chuhng-doo | **Loshan** | Loh-shahn |
| **Chiang Kaishek** | Jee-ahng Ki-shek | **Luchow** | Loo-joh |
| **Chiaochetu** | Jee-ao-jeh-doo | **Mao Tsetung** | Mao Dzuh-doong |
| **Chinghai** | Ching-hi | **Mekong** | May-kong |
| **Chinkiang** | Jin-jee-ahng | **Miao** | Mee-ao |
| **Chinsha Kiang** | Jin-shah Jee-ahng | **Min** | Min |
| **Chungking** | Chuhng-ching | **Ming** | Ming |
| **Chu Shan** | Choo Shahn | **Nanking** | Nahn-jing |
| **Dri Chu** | Dree Choo | **Nantung** | Nahn-tuhng |
| **Formosa** | For-moh-sah | **Nasi** | Nah-shee |
| **Han** | Hahn | **Neikang** | Nay-jee-ahng |
| **Hangchow** | Hahng-joh | **Peking** | Bay-jing |
| **Hankow** | Hahn-koh | **Pohai** | Boh-hi |
| **Hanyang** | Hahn-yahng | **Poyang** | Poh-yahng |
| **Hunan** | Hoo-nahn | **Shang** | Shahng |
| **Hwang Pu** | Huahng-poo | **Shanghai** | Shahng-hi |
| **Hweitseh** | Whay-dzuh | **Shao Shan** | Shao Shahn |
| **Ichang** | Ee-chahng | **Shuba** | Shuh-ba |
| **Ipin** | Ee-pin | **Siang Kiang** | Shee-ahng Jeeahng |
| **Jyekundo** | Jueh-kuhn-doh | **Soochow** | Soo-chao |
| **Kansu** | Kahn-soo | **Sun Yat-sen** | Soon Yaht-sen |
| **Kham** | Khahm | **Szechwan** | Suh-chwahn |
| **Khamba** | Khahm-bah | **Taiwan** | Ti-wahn |
| **Kialing** | Jee-ah-ling | **Tibet** | Tih-bet |
| **Kienwei** | Jee-en-way | **To Kiang** | Toh Jee-ahng |
| **Kingkiang** | Jing-jee-ahng | **tsamba** | tsahm-ba |
| **Kokoshili** | Koh-koh-shee-lee | **tung** | tuhng |
| **Kunming** | Kuhn-ming | **Tungting** | Duhng-ting |
| **lama** | lahmuh | **Tzechung** | Dzuh-juhng |
| **lamasery** | lah-muh-sair-ee | **Wuchang** | Woo-chahng |
| **Lhasa** | Lhah-sah | **Wuhan** | Woo-hahn |
| **Li Erh-lang** | Lee Erh-lahng | **Wuhsia** | Woo-shee-a |

| WORD | PRONUNCIATION | WORD | PRONUNCIATION |
|------|---------------|------|---------------|
| Wu Hsien | Woo Shee-ehn | Yenan | Yen-ahn |
| Wuhu | Woo-hoo | Yi | Yee |
| Wutungkiao | Woo-tuhng-jee-ao | Yumen | Yoo-muhn |
| Yalung | Yah-luhng | Yunnan | Yuhn-nahn |
| Yangtze Kiang | Yahng-dzuh Jee-ahng | Yushu | Yoo-shoo |

# INDEX